Original title:
The Aroma of Thanksgiving Dinner

Author: Samuel Kensington

ISBN HARDBACK: 978-9916-94-358-8
ISBN PAPERBACK: 978-9916-94-359-5

Family Gathered Round

In the kitchen, chaos reigns,
The dog snatches a ham, then it trains.
A cousin drops the cranberry jar,
'Tis the season for mishaps, so bizarre!

Auntie's recipe calls for a dash,
She adds a pinch, but makes a splash.
Uncle Fred insists on extra spice,
We'll need a fire extinguisher, how nice!

Maple-Glazed Whispers

Sweet scents waft through the air,
Uncle Joe claims he's the best chef fair.
Grandma shouts, 'That's too much glaze!'
It's becoming a sticky, syrupy maze!

Cousins giggle as they sneak a bite,
'Is that the pie or a gooey site?'
Laughter rings as veggies dance,
Will the turkey provide a second chance?

The Essence of Togetherness

Gathered near, we share our tales,
With turkey tales that often fail.
Mom burns the rolls, Dad saves the day,
His charred offering? Hooray, hooray!

Sister sneezes, and the pie takes flight,
Smashing on Grandma, quite a sight!
Laughter erupts, and the dogs all cheer,
Dinner's a circus, oh what a year!

A Symphony of Savories

The table's set with strange delight,
Casseroles glowing like a fright.
Cousin's concoction has an odd hue,
'What is that, is it edible too?'

The stuffing sings a questionable tune,
As pie slices dance beneath the moon.
Belly laughs and awkward cheers,
We feast on love, with silly sneers!

Hints of Maple and Cranberry

A turkey on the table, what a sight,
Gravy rivers flow, oh, what pure delight!
Potatoes in a mountain, soft and creamy,
The kids plot to steal, oh so dreamy!

Cranberry sauce in a jiggly form,
Who knew pink could be so much fun to swarm?
Maple drizzles making everyone cheer,
'Pass the syrup!' they shout, loud and clear!

Embraces Wrapped in Warmth

Sweaters snug like mashed potatoes blend,
Chili in the air, a feast to commend!
Grandma's secret pie, so sweet and grand,
Saving some for later, oh, that was the plan!

With each bite taken, laughter rings out,
Who dropped the rolls? Can they go without a pout?
Uncles argue football, wine glass in hand,
While tots giggle, thinking it all unplanned!

Cozy Hearth and Spiced Air

A blaze in the hearth, warmth all around,
Spiced pumpkin delights, oh my, do abound!
Dancing shadows flicker, stories unwind,
Every table tale is perfectly designed!

The cat steals the turkey, a furry crook,
Wagging his tail, as the family cooks.
Laughter erupts, it's a comedy line,
Who knew dinner could feel so divine?

Essence of Home and Hearth

Every corner filled with joyous cheer,
Laughter and chatter, what a great year!
Kids playing tag in a snug little space,
While pie-eyed grandpa sports whipped cream on his
face!

Eggnog spills over, stains on the floor,
Seems holiday spirits brought merry galore!
With puns about stuffing filling the air,
Thanksgiving's a riot, and we're glad to share!

An Invitation to Feast

Come one, come all, to our grand table,
Where turkey legs dance, if they're able.
Stuffing whispers secrets from their bowl,
And cranberry sauce claims it's on a roll!

With pies that giggle, they steal the show,
Pumpkin and pecan, oh, don't be slow!
Grab a plate, but mind the gravy tide,
For mashed potatoes refuse to hide!

The Fragrance of Togetherness

Oh, the scents swirling, like a comedy play,
Sweet potatoes sass even though they're gray.
Green beans gossip, while rolls rise and puff,
Let's hope the kitchen's strong enough for the stuff!

Laughter erupts over spilled cranberry,
A troop of peas marching, oh so merry.
Grandma's in charge, as she howls with glee,
Mixing her dishes with a splash of tea!

Culinary Dreams Unfold

In the oven, dreams are baking bright,
But watch out for that turkey—it's ready to fight!
Mashed potatoes huddle, they're feeling quite bold,
Each spoonful cries, 'We're better when sold!'

Cornbread's a rebel, trying to be sweet,
Teasing the butter, "Come dance on my heat!"
Pies line up, wearing crusty hats,
Winking at forks, saying, "Let's have some chats!"

Fresh Baked Joy

Out comes the bread, looking puffed and proud,
Making the whole kitchen burst like a cloud.
The cookies are near, with a smile on their face,
Jumping in jars, saying, "Let's find our place!"

Lemon meringue shouts, "I'm zesty, not shy!"
While pumpkin pie winks, and gives it a try.
Happy bellies grumble, the feast has begun,
As laughter mixes with butter, oh what fun!

An Invitation to Indulge

Join us at the table, oh what a sight,
Turkey and stuffing, a pure delight.
Gravy like rivers, flowing all around,
Pies stack so high, no room left unbound.

Pass the sweet potatoes, they're covered in fluff,
"Just one more bite," you'll say, but it's tough.
Unbutton those pants, you'll need some reprieve,
This feast is a trap, you won't want to leave.

Fragrant Bounty

Turkey's poppers dance with glee,
Stuffing whispers, "Come feast with me!"
Lurking greens say, "We're not mean!"
Mashing potatoes, they start to scream.

A pie emerges, steaming and round,
Pumpkin spice wafts—what's that sound?
Uncle Joe's jokes, a little flat,
But oh, that cranberry splat!

Chasing Flavorful Echoes

We chase tasty whispers, on a savory quest,
Pies calling our names, couldn't ask for more zest.
Lost in a sea of gravy and cheese,
The turkey starts dancing, "Is that a disease?"

Laughter erupts, as the yams start to roll,
When dad goes for seconds, he loses control.
With every big burp comes a round of applause,
This feast is a riot; it breaks all the laws!

Dances of Spice

Smells waltz through the air, a cha-cha of zest,
Herbs shimmy and shake, giving flavors their best.
Cinnamon twirls, and pepper spins round,
As garlic kicks off a funk, oh, what a sound!

Potatoes in rhythm, mashed with a beat,
While the salad greens sway, they can't stay discreet.
When pie takes a bow, the crowd bursts in cheer,
Just don't ask for seconds—oh dear, oh dear!

Embracing the Feast

Gather round the spread, what a funny scene,
Cousin Bob's mishap with the cranberry bean.
He tried to impress with his culinary flair,
But now it's a war with the cat on a chair.

Pumpkin pie giggles as it wobbles in place,
While grandpa tells stories, with crumbs on his face.
"More rolls?" mutters uncle, with butter in hand,
He's in a love affair; it's simply unplanned.

Spice-Kissed Memories

Grandma's hands, a sprinkle of zest,
Her secret blend, we all want to test.
Orange peels collide with a wink,
Spices jumping—oh, what do you think?

The cousin's dance, a wild buffet,
Eating too much, we laugh and sway.
The dog eyes us from the rug,
Hoping for scraps, he's such a chug!

Hearthside Harmony

Chatterbox aunts with stories to share,
They claim the turkey could dance in midair.
Fried green beans in a casserole hug,
Sibling rivalry, we'll pull and tug!

Laughter fills the air, it's pure delight,
Dad's prank game turns serious tonight.
Mom says, "No more, we can't possibly eat!"
Then dessert rolls out—what a sweet treat!

Cranberry Dreams

Jiggly cranberry, what's that delight?
It's wobbly and weird, but oh, what a sight!
Relatives squish it on bread with a grin,
While cousins sneak bites, laughter within.

The feast finally ends, but tales are still spun,
Awkward dance-offs, boy, was that fun!
Sleepy faces, but hunger's not done,
Guess we'll save room for turkey rerun!

Turkeys in the Twilight

Turkeys wander, gobbling with flair,
As they plot their escape, beyond the chair.
The stuffing laughs, in a buttery dress,
While pies conspire, seeking sweet success.

Uncle Bob trips, while trying to dance,
Knocking over gravy, lost in a trance.
The rolls start rolling, in a floury race,
As everyone smiles, their worries erase.

A Feast of Warmth

Grandma's in charge, with her secret stash,
Whipping up dishes, with a magical dash.
Potatoes are mashed, with butter so bright,
While cousins sneak snacks, in the soft, dim light.

Vegetables tumble, in a colorful show,
The cranberry sauce races, like it's in the know.
With laughter and cheers, the table's a sight,
As tummies all rumble, ready for a bite.

Cinnamon and Cloves

Time to spice up, with cinnamon's kiss,
As pumpkin pie warms, in oven's sweet bliss.
Cloves whisper secrets, through each fragrant bake,
Turkey looks nervous, oh for goodness' sake!

Laughter erupts, when the cat makes a dash,
Snatching sweet rolls, oh what a splash!
With everyone giggling, it's quite the display,
As the feast keeps growing, who's hungry? Okay!

Blessings on the Plate

Gather 'round folks, it's that time of year,
With jests and great cheers, let's all draw near.
Each plate a blessing, with love piled high,
As children make faces, and corn starts to fly.

The dog makes a plea, with his big puppy eyes,
While Aunt Cora tells tales, much to our surprise.
With forks raised in triumph, we dive into glee,
In this feast of warmth, we're as happy as can be.

Sage and Comfort

Sage sprinkled across the big, brown bird,
A fragrance that just can't be deferred.
The dog is dreaming of a turkey slice,
While we debate who's serving up the rice.

Grandma's rolling dough, what a funny sight,
With flour flying left, and a dash to the right.
The oven's beeping like a comedy show,
Who knew this meal would start a food throw?

Roasted Remembrances

Grandpa tells tales that make us all cringe,
As he carves the turkey with a mischievous grin.
Remember the time he mistook salt for sugar?
That dish was a true dining room juggernaut!

The pie is so sweet, it made the kids dance,
With whipped cream piled high, it's a sugary trance.
A spoon drops to the floor, and laughter erupts,
Thanksgiving's the time for both stuffing and pups.

A Cornucopia of Love

A table so full, you need a compass,
With green bean casserole and cheesy euphoria.
Uncle Bob's eating like he's in a race,
We all just stare, it's a unique embrace.

Mashed potatoes mountain, rich and creamy,
The kids are asking, "Are we dreaming, really?"
As gravy spills, it's a cartoonish scene,
With laughter blooming like the veggie cuisine.

Candied Hopes

Sweet potatoes topped with marshmallow fluff,
Sometimes you wonder if they've overstuffed.
But Auntie's smile makes everything divine,
Even if her cooking looks borderline!

The kids are busy with their wild charades,
While we sip cider and throw food grenades.
A toast to this time, filled with flavors galore,
Each bite a memory, and we just want more!

Harvest Whispers

As turkeys dance on kitchen floors,
The gravy spills like ancient wars.
Pumpkin pies with cheeky grins,
A feast begins, let laughter win.

A clumsy chef with floury hands,
Dropped the rolls, oh how it stands!
Cranberry sauce like a splattered art,
We feast together, a foodie heart.

The table groans with dishes vast,
Sweet potatoes sing, the die is cast.
Naps are planned, but first, we cheer,
For every bite brings holiday cheer!

So grab your fork, and start to munch,
Remember, leftovers, always the punch!
Thanksgiving fun, it's quite a sight,
Together we dine, with hearts so light.

Spice-Scented Memories

In the oven, pies loudly sing,
As grandpa talks about his bling.
Stuffing spills with a joyous crack,
While the dogs plan an epic snack.

The yams go missing, where could they be?
In the cat's paws, oh woe is me!
Dinner rolls doing a little dance,
Can't resist a second chance!

The laughter rises, the jokes get bold,
Who knew mashed potatoes could unfold?
With every bite, the stories brew,
Creating memories, both old and new.

So here we are, plates piled high,
With every scoop, a shared reply.
Thanksgiving shenanigans, oh so grand,
We'll eat our way through this wonderland.

A Feast of Fragrant Delights

A turkey trumpets from the roast,
While kids plan how to boast.
Gravy rivers, take a dip,
Watch the brussel sprouts do a flip!

Grandma's secret recipe is a tease,
With an ingredient that promises to please.
Cinnamon hugs the autumn air,
While burnt toast gives us quite the scare.

The cranberry splash makes quite a mess,
On the dog's tail, oh what duress!
Laughter echoes, as pies deflate,
We cheerfully celebrate our plate!

With every bite, a giggle springs,
In this banquet of love, joy sings.
So let's raise a glass and make a toast,
For every cherished moment we love most.

Scented Traditions

The kitchen buzzes, flavors collide,
Mom's on a mission, can't let it slide.
Potatoes whirlpool in a buttery dance,
Can't resist the carbs, not a chance!

Cranberries popping like confetti bright,
While dad tries to set the turkey right.
His secret weapon? A YouTube guide,
Instructions gone, now he just hides!

Under the table, a food fight blooms,
With forks as swords and laughter in rooms.
The rolls are weapons, the gravy's a shield,
In this culinary battlefield, none will yield.

As dinner ends, the pie's a delight,
With sweet whispers as we take flight.
Thanksgiving fun, it's clear to see,
Together in chaos, we let it be.

Unity in Every Dish

In the kitchen, pots collide,
Mom's stuffing is a fun ride.
Cousin Joe makes gravy splash,
Uncle Bob just burnt his hash.

Turkey struts with cranberry grace,
Pumpkin pie in a pie-faced race.
Sister's salad—brought last minute,
Who knew we'd need a green spinach wit?

Everyone's juggling flavors bold,
Together we make a tale retold.
Laughter rises, the table's a sight,
Thanksgiving chaos, what a delight!

So we feast and we joke and we play,
Each dish brings its own little flair.
In this mishmash of blitz and whim,
Unity shines, amidst the din.

A Palette of Thankfulness

Carrots dance in a butter bath,
While Aunt Sue stirs the veggie wrath.
"Is it sweet or a bit too bland?"
Someone cries, "It's from dry land!"

Potatoes pile with a salty cheer,
Who knew they'd end up so near?
"Not too lumpy!" is Grandma's decree,
But we secretly cheer for a lump or three.

Like a painter, we mix and blend,
Each dish a canvas that we mend.
With every taste, a chuckle more,
Thankful hearts in a flavor war!

So raise a glass to all things bright,
From salads dressed to rolls in flight.
A quirky feast, oh what a thrill,
Together we savor every spill!

Feast of Generations

Gather 'round the table's spread,
Where Grandpa's tales make us all dread.
"Did I ever tell you 'bout that time?"
We nod and laugh at his nose's grime.

The kids are plotting a pie heist,
While Aunties engage in cake slice feist.
"More green beans!" someone yells in glee,
Only to find the dish is empty!

Memories mixed with butter and spice,
Family secrets served on a slice.
Echoes of laughter, both loud and sweet,
At this feast, it's never discreet!

So we cherish traditions age-old,
While passing dishes far from controlled.
Each generation, a slice of fun,
In this culinary race, we're all winners—everyone!

Melodies of the Kitchen

In the kitchen, music plays,
As pots and pans join in the frays.
"Watch the gravy!" warns the chef,
But cousin Tim just made a mess.

With every chop and every stir,
A symphony of scents occurs.
The turkey sings a soulful tune,
While biscuits rise beneath the moon.

Custards slide like dancers fine,
As pies perform, a choreographed line.
A chorus of friends, a feast divine,
In laughter's echo, our spirits shine.

So here's to flavors, big and small,
As we gather 'round, there's room for all.
In this kitchen, love's a hit,
With every note, we're bonded—bit by bit!

Gathering of Aromatic Whispers

Turkey's in the oven, on a road to fame,
Cranberry sauce wrestling for its name.
Pumpkin pie is winking, with a cheeky grin,
While the stuffing giggles at the turkey's sin.

Gravy boats are sailing, with a splash and a plop,
Mashed potatoes acting like they're ready to hop.
Rolls are bouncing merrily, soft and round,
As the green beans plot to cause a sound.

Families convene, it's a tasty parade,
Uncles debating which dish they have made.
Auntie's secret recipe, she swears it's divine,
But cousin Bob's burnt toast is crossing the line.

Laughter fills the air, as diners unite,
Over pots of delight, a comical sight.
Belly laughs cascade, with every surprise,
As we feast on fun, with giggles and sighs.

Hearth and Heart

Gathered around in the cozy warm light,
The turkey once martial, now a comical sight.
Grandma's casseroles, a roguish delight,
Begin their takeover with each bite in flight.

Pies stare mischievously, fresh from the bake,
Will they take flight, or just make a mistake?
Kids whisper secrets, while we toil away,
As the sweet potato sings, 'I'm the star today!'

Dad spills the gravy, a comical splash,
And cousin Sue giggles, all dressed up in trash.
Uncle Jerry's cornbread, a rock in disguise,
Looks ready to launch, right up to the skies.

So we raise a toast, with soda in hand,
"To family and food, isn't it grand?"
With laughter and love, we all play our parts,
In the heart of the hearth, where warmth never departs.

The Gathering's Essence

A feast laid out, oh what a grand spread,
With turkey so juicy, it's blushingly red.
Potatoes are mashed like my goofy old friend,
Who claims he will diet right after this blend.

Cranberry giggles, a tart little tease,
While yams in the oven release 'eat me' pleas.
Everyone's hungry, and laughter's the key,
To survive Uncle Bob's loud jubilee.

Outside the kitchen, I hear rumbles galore,
Is it stomach grumbling, or Grandma's floor?
With every "Who's hungry?" the chaos ignites,
And forks are like missiles in lively food fights.

Yet here's the essence, amidst food and fun,
Bonding and banter, a race to be won.
For in every dish lies a story, a cheer,
In gatherings scented with love, laughter, and beer.

Celebration in the Air

Dinner bells ring, oh what a commotion,
With pies flying high like a food-based notion.
Mom's in the kitchen, her hair all awry,
As dad drops the turkey with a woeful sigh.

Chairs squeak and shuffle, as we take a seat,
A salad's envious of the turkey's full feat.
Broccoli's fuming, it just wants a bite,
While the cranberry sauce is ready to fight.

Aunt says, "More rolls!" with a dramatic flair,
Uncle just nods, like he hasn't a care.
With laughter and stories, the room fills up fast,
As we savor our dinner, till we're really quite past.

So raise up your glasses, here's to the fun,
To family and friendship, we've only begun!
This celebration, with each flavor and cheer,
Leaves us with joy, till next yearly year!

Boiling Broths and Shared Stories

The pot is bubbling, oh what a sight,
Grandma's secret spice smells just right.
Uncle Joe's jokes are just a tad stale,
But we all laugh like we're on a fun trail.

Cousin Billy thinks he can cook,
But his dish looks like a mystery book.
Mom just smiles, her apron so stained,
Cooking skills, at least, she has trained.

A toast of cider with a gagging twist,
Someone's diet? They can't resist!
We sip and giggle, stories unfold,
At a table where jokes are gold.

Pie descends like a sweetened cloud,
Slicing into laughter, we feel so proud.
As crumbs scatter like confetti around,
We cheer for the feast, our joy unbound.

Thanksgiving Whimsy

Turkey-shaped cookies, the kids go wild,
Mashed potatoes that look like a child!
A feast of flavors, each weird and whacky,
Who knew cooking could feel so tacky?

A dog under the table hopes for a crumb,
While the cat lies in wait, looking so dumb.
"Who put raisins in the stuffing?" we shout,
As Mom winks, plotting her next tricky route.

The kids all squabble over who gets more,
While Aunt Sally insists, "There's always a score!"
We're stuffed to the gills, yet still eye dessert,
"It's practically a sin to pass up on that skirt."

The evening winds down with a cozy snore,
The pumpkin pie's gone, and we all want more.
With belly aches shared and laughter unrolls,
Thanksgiving's the time for our heart and our souls.

Table of Thankful Hearts

At the table, we gather, looking quite spry,
Turkey's been carved, oh my, oh my!
The stuffing's a mix, a curious blend,
To be honest, we might need to amend.

A toast is raised, glass clinks in cheer,
"Here's to family!" we shout, loud and clear.
In this chaotic feast, stories ignite,
And Uncle Tom claims he's ready to fight.

Grandpa's asleep, the turkey's still hot,
His snores are the soundtrack, why worry a lot?
With laughter cascading, our hearts feel so light,
In a world of gratitude, everything feels right.

As we savor the pie, and the evening grows late,
Mom takes the reins, "Let's clean up the plate!"
But before we can start, a dance breaks the mold,
Thankful hearts living brightly, stories retold.

Nostalgic Notes of Nourishment

At the table, the food arrives,
Old recipes bring sweet surprise,
A chorus of flavors starts to play,
With each bite, we dream away.

Potatoes whisper tales from the past,
While sweet corn dances, a spell is cast,
A bit of humor, a chef's delight,
Just hope that towel doesn't ignite!

There's stuffing hidden like a secret treasure,
In every bite, a sense of pleasure,
Family together, a quirky clan,
Who makes up recipes in a unique plan.

In pots and pans, laughter's light,
We feast 'til the morn or late at night,
Nostalgia served on a fancy dish,
With every bite, we find our wish.

Feasting Under the Harvest Moon

Turkey wobbles on the plate,
As grandma's pies start to skate.
Cranberries dance with zestful flair,
Uncle Joe's snoring fills the air.

Gravy spills like a river wide,
The cat plots a tasty slide.
Sourdough rolls are on a roll,
While cousins fight for the last bowl.

Laughter echoes, a joyful sound,
As mashed potatoes hit the ground.
Leftovers stacked high like a tower,
Oh, the joy of mealtime power!

With every bite, a giggle bursts,
For dessert, we face our worst.
Pumpkin pie, a spicy thrill,
But first, let's conquer that last meal!

Tender Moments Shared

Gather round the festive table,
Fond memories linger, oh so stable,
Auntie's jokes, we roll our eyes,
But in her heart, she surely tries.

Turkey legs with a sous-chef dance,
Join in for a food-loving prance,
Grandpa's stories of days gone by,
Did he really see a flying pie?

Pie fights break with a cheeky grin,
A whipped cream cap from brother's chin,
Laughter bounces off the walls,
As we revel in our holiday brawls.

Mom holds her breath, has a near call,
While juggling dishes, she could trip and fall,
Yet with one last dash, she grins so wide,
In these tender moments, we all take pride.

Stuffed Hearts and Cider

With every sip of cider sweet,
We toast to all the things we eat,
Grandma's recipe, a secret pass,
Does anyone know what's in that glass?

Stuffing, oh the crafty clay,
Is it bread or did it play?
A hint of sage or just the spice,
I swear it winked at me—how nice!

A turkey trots, it starts to sing,
Who knew birds could do such a thing?
While cousins chase the dog for fun,
Only to lose, oh what a run!

Hearts are full, and bellies too,
Laughter plays like a joyful tune,
Let's pile more food upon our plates,
And tell dad to stop sharing his dates!

A Journey Through Flavor

In the kitchen, pots are racing,
Turkey's got a funny face,
Cranberry sauce, oh what a sight,
Green beans dancing, pure delight.

Gravy flows like a river wide,
Mashed potatoes poised with pride,
Rolls are puffing up with glee,
Who knew food could have such a spree?

Pumpkin pie with a whipped cream hat,
Kids in a food coma, just like that,
When the feast begins, the laughter spills,
And Uncle Bob brings one of his 'skills'.

So grab a plate, let's celebrate,
With silly hats, let's elevate,
Joy found in every spoon and fork,
Why does that turkey look at me and smirk?

Bountiful Blessings

With dishes so plenty, the table does groan,
Who knew cooking could feel like a throne?
A casserole here and a pie over there,
Grandma's baked beans have a smell beyond compare.

The kids are in mischief, oh what a sight,
One's got a fork, and it's quite the fright!
Pass the potatoes, just watch the fight,
To eat or to laugh? Both feel just right.

Uncle Dave's stories take way too long,
"Fast forward to pie!" is our favorite song.
As we stuff our faces, a food coma creeps,
With recipes whispered and giggles, we leap.

The pumpkin's been plundered, the cranberry's gone,
As dessert rolls in, oh sweet goodness dawn!
We laugh through the feasting, our spirits are bright,
Giving thanks for each bite in this feast of delight.

Home for the Holidays

The kitchen hums a merry tune,
As doorbells chime, we're home by noon.
Sweet potato soufflé, a sticky mess,
Can't wait to taste, I must confess.

Auntie's cookies, burnt just right,
Dad's jokes land with a comical bite.
Snowflakes fall like confetti bright,
While turkey's tender, a glorious sight.

Grandpa's chair won't make it through,
With every laugh, we drop our stew.
Naps are planned for the food that's served,
Best keep the ice cream in reserve!

Hugs and pies, a feast of cheer,
As we gather everyone near.
With a toast that'll shake the floor,
Here's to laughter, forevermore!

Comfort in Each Bite

A pot of stew whirls with delight,
Disguising veggies in a meaty fight.
With every bite, a gag reflex grows,
Who added garlic? Nobody knows!

The turkey's antics steal the show,
Dancing on the table, bold and slow.
Sweet rolls whisper, 'We're still alive,'
As kids jump up, 'Let our bellies thrive!'

Gravy rivers, cascading down,
Will this feast earn us a crown?
Stuffing's got a life of its own,
We're crowning a king made of scone!

Leftover dreams are now a hoot,
With mashed potatoes serving as loot.
In this chaos, we all unite,
With giggles tucked in, it feels just right!

Saplings and Savories

The veggies spring up in a dance,
As mashed roots give potatoes a chance.
Pumpkins roll with a smile so grand,
While harvest hues paint every hand.

Cousins compete for the pie slice prize,
A showdown of hunger and gluttonous eyes.
Broccoli flirts, all dressed in cheese,
While grandpa snoozes with surprising ease.

Beneath the table, the cat's in the fray,
With turkey leg just a paw's away.
We aim for a feast that's loud and bright,
With flavors mingling in pure delight.

So here's to the joy of each dish and bite,
A belly full of laughter feels just right.
In a whirlwind of tastes, we find our tune,
As we feast beneath the harvest moon!

Soothing Scents of Tradition

A pot's bubbling laughter fills the air,
Turkey's in trouble, it's quite a scare!
Pumpkin pie whispers, "Slice me with flair,"
Mashed potatoes grinning, ready to share.

Green beans dancing, they sashay about,
Gravy is slick, like a smooth, sly scout!
Rolls are a-jiggling, with buddies devout,
Dinner's a circus, with fun all throughout.

Cranberries jostle, sweet-tart in the mix,
Who needs a diet? Just hand me the fix!
Everyone munches, relying on tricks,
Eating's a sport, and we're pros, can't you fix?

As laughter erupts like a wild confetti,
We toast to the chaos, our plates getting petty!
Facing the leftovers, oh boy, what's the betty?
Our stomachs are full, and yet there's more ready!

Woven Together by Flavor

Threads of spices tightly entwined,
Tasting each dish, with pleasure aligned.
A feast of delights, so sweet and undefined,
Who knew that for seconds, we'd all be resigned?

Stuffing's a hug, all cozy and warm,
Granny's old recipe takes on new charm.
A turkey so juicy, you'd think it was farmed,
While relatives bicker—no one's alarmed!

On the table, a colorful riot,
Fried onions on green beans, can't keep quiet!
Holiday spirit, this cook's secret diet,
In the cornucopia, we all feel the fly it!

Desserts come rolling in, one after another,
Sweet pot pie making us cheer for our mother.
Calories call, making us all shudder,
But with fun and laughter, we'll never blunder!

Candles and Culinary Creations

Candles flicker, with scents so divine,
While Uncle Joe claims he's a chef with a line.
"Just add more butter!" he shouts like a sign,
The dinner's exploding—it's a quaint time!

Tables adorned with plates piled so high,
We'll feast like kings with food floating nigh.
With festive shenanigans, we laugh till we cry,
While cousin Sue swears she's learning to fry!

Kitchen's a madhouse, a laugh riot reigns,
Pies wobble and giggle, defying all chains.
As we serve up gratitude through our silly campaigns,
Every mouthful's a journey—like running on trains!

Candles are dancing, and so is the crew,
As Grandpa shares stories, some terribly true.
Thanksgiving is here, with love to brew,
Amidst all the laughter, we cherish the view!

Gratitude Served Warm

Gathered around, the family arrives,
With comical tales that spark silly jives.
A pot roast giggles as sauce takes dives,
And everyone munches, exploring the hives.

The sweet and the savory, friends so close,
Stuffing that hugs like a fave little ghost.
Cranberry highs—yes, there's nothing gross,
While Auntie Fern's pie gives us all a toast!

Giggles abound while desserts collide,
With flavors and friendships we cannot divide.
Each plate full of laughter, plus a side of pride,
And love served warm, on this wild dinner ride!

As dinner wraps up, we share silly cheers,
Jokes about jumpy turkeys start to appear.
Grateful for moments, through laughter and tears,
Our feast is the best, year after year!

Ode to Roasted Richness

Golden bird on display, oh what a sight,
Dripping juices that shimmer, much to my delight.
The sides all conspire in a buttery dance,
Even the gravy, wearing its best pants.

Potatoes piled high like a mountainous dream,
With crispy edges that make my heart beam.
Stuffing so rich, it could rock a small boat,
And pie that could easily win a sweet vote.

Cranberries bobbing like little red pearls,
While my waistline expands, making great swirls.
Oh, how we feast, the laughter's the star,
With jokes flying high like we're under a bar.

So gather, oh friends, let us munch and weep,
For these glorious dishes, my heart they will keep.
In this joyous chaos, let joy intertwine,
With seconds and thirds, we all drink the wine.

The Warmth of Culinary Comfort

In the corner, the rolls are puffing up high,
Like fluffy little clouds that will soon say goodbye.
But beware of the butter, it's slippery and sly,
One bite too many, and oh me, oh my!

Green beans all jazzed with a crispy old crunch,
And let's not forget about the sweet potato bunch.
Marshmallows on top like a sugary summit,
One forkful away from a delightful plummet.

The table a battlefield, plates piled with pride,
While out in the hall, the toddlers collide.
Uncles with stories, they really can babble,
Around the feast, it's all giggles and gabble.

A feast to remember, oh what a delight,
With love in each bite and laughter in sight.
So let's pass those dishes, the laughter will flow,
And the joy of this season will always aglow.

Pine and Sage in the Air

Pine needles freshly swept on this festive ground,
While the sage leaves a scent that's quite profound.
A kitchen brigade stirring pots like a show,
The turkey's in there, giving everyone a glow.

The pies are all cooling on window's embrace,
Dreaming of weekends in a sugar-filled race.
Pumpkin and pecan, ready for their crown,
With whipped cream atop to keep the smiles abound.

Relatives gather with stories they bring,
Fables of past feats, oh what joy they all sing!
The laughter erupts, like a bubbling brew,
As the cat eyes the turkey, plotting his coup.

So raise up your glasses, let's toast to this day,
For the love in each dish, in a scrumptious array.
With a wink and a grin, let's savor the cheer,
For the feast and the fun; it's that time of year!

Savory Encounters

The clock strikes twelve, and the aromas collide,
As vegetables dance with the turkey beside.
Spices are swirling like a merry old game,
Each bite tells a story, none ever the same.

Chopping and stirring, it's a culinary clatter,
While kids play tag in a friendly old patter.
I sneak a quick bit, hoping no one will see,
But a rogue green bean jumps right onto me!

Grandma's brisket is famous, a legend so bold,
While Uncle Bob's antics are worth their weight in gold.
You'd think we were racing, the way that we feast,
Just one more helping? Oh yes, just a least!

With plates piled high, laughter fills up the room,
While desserts are prepared for a sugar-filled boom.
So we gather around, grateful hearts in full swing,
In this joyous mayhem, let the festivities ring!

Feast of Essential Scents

In the kitchen pots start to dance,
Garlic and onions in a fragrant trance.
Turkeys strutting, surrounded by cheer,
Pumpkin pie grinning, it's that time of year.

Mom's secret spice sends the dog on a quest,
While Uncle Fred snoozes, dressed in his best.
Gravy's a river, flowing so thick,
Who knew green beans could vanish so quick?

The cranberry jelly, it's wobbly and bright,
Makes the perfect target for the cat's delight.
Everyone's hungry, the table's a sight,
But Auntie's lost the rolls again, oh what a fright!

Thanksgiving's a circus, full of flavors and glee,
With cousin Tim's jokes, as bad as can be.
Yet, despite all the chaos and mad, we agree,
It's the laughter and love that makes it key.

Savory Journeys

Turkey takes flight on a spicy delight,
The kids are all shouting, 'It's time to unite!'
Sweet potatoes marching, in marshmallow coats,
While Dad tries to juggle—oh, not his best quote.

A dash of confusion, a sprinkle of fun,
While Grandma battles the Brussel sprouts run.
The smell of the stuffing, a carb-laden song,
It's the dinner table dance, where we all belong.

Mmm, the pie crust rebels, it won't be outdone,
A feast of tradition, and family—oh, fun!
With cousin Joe's antics, we all share a laugh,
As the dog sneaks a slice, oh boy, what a gaffe!

Dinner rolls hug butter as friends start to bicker,
Uncle's tall tales make the hour feel quicker.
In this savory journey, with hearts full and spread,
It's more than just cooking, it's love that we tread.

Connection Through Cuisine

Mashed potatoes fluff up like clouds in the sky,
As the green bean casserole gives a sly wink and a sigh.
Together at the table, all flavors unite,
Like wild family stories that take off in flight.

A fork flies through the air, as Aunt Sue takes a bite,
While Dad's dancing in place, thinking he's quite the sight.
The stuffing's a masterpiece, claimed as a win,
Though covered in gravy, it beggars the skin.

With laughter like butter, it spreads through the room,
While cousin Bob tells tales that lead to our doom.
Cranberries wobble, in jelly-like ways,
As we count our blessings and share all our praise.

Amidst all the banter, the flavors collide,
In connection through cuisine, we take great pride.
As the last slice of pie teeters close to the edge,
It's the love that we feast on, our heart's golden pledge.

Savoring the Season

In the corner the squash glimmers, thinking it's fine,
While pie takes the spotlight—oh, what a design!
Turkey's so golden, it speaks to the crowd,
As Aunt Jane's famous punch goes wild and loud!

Savoring flavors that shout with delight,
Siblings throwing bread rolls in a comical fight.
Apple cider bubbling, a frothy delight,
Grandpa's tall tales soar higher than height!

Oh, the sweet scent of cinnamon dances around,
While kids sneak the stuffing, without making a sound.
With laughter that echoes, and hearts that are free,
We cherish the moments, as tasty as can be.

So we raise up our glasses, and toast to this cheer,
For the season of feasting, it brings us all near.
It's the silly, the merry, the flavors we share,
That fills up our souls with a love beyond compare.

Tasteful Thanksgiving Reflections

The turkey's dancing on the plate,
With gravy waves that captivate.
Mashed potatoes, fluffy clouds,
Whispering secrets, laughter loud.

Cranberry sauce, a jiggly blob,
Telling tales of every job.
Green beans strewn like tiny spears,
Standing tall through all our cheers.

Pumpkin pie, a sweet delight,
With whipped cream peaks that take to flight.
Uncles argue, who's the best cook?
While kids just nod and flee the nook.

With plates piled high, we all partake,
Selfies snapped, the turkey shakes.
As laughter swells and glasses clink,
We toast to food and what we think!

Rustic Gatherings and Hidden Flavors

Around the table, all faces cheer,
While Auntie's casserole draws a sneer.
Burnt edges hide good intentions,
Leading to strange culinary tensions.

Grandpa's jokes are stale like bread,
Yet everyone laughs till tears are shed.
A feast of flavors, so much to savor,
Even the pet dog is a food slaver.

Stuffing's a mystery, bound to confound,
As cousins debate its origin sound.
With spoons like swords, we wage our fight,
Over who steals the last big bite.

Kitchen aromas, a fragrant brawl,
The warrior chefs, we'll answer the call.
To bask in laughter, and gobble with glee,
Thankful for family and all that we see.

A Canvas of Culinary Love

The table's set with mismatched plates,
Bringing flavors from distant fates.
Pecan pie winks with a nutty grin,
While sweet potatoes sing, 'Dive right in!'

Sisters giggle over who'll do the dishes,
As uncles plot their midnight wishes.
Rolls round like a toddler on the floor,
'Eat it slow, there's always more!'

Mother's stuffing lands with a thud,
It's supposed to be cooked, not in mud!
Yet all's forgiven with pumpkin spice,
As we feast and scatter crumbs like mice.

Drinks in hand, we make our toast,
To loved ones near and those we miss most.
In this pixelated food gallery,
We embrace chaos with savory salary.

The Gathering of Flavors

Gather round, the feast is here,
With dishes that bring both joy and fear.
The turkey's grandeur, a sight to behold,
Like a royal crow, it struts bold.

Gravy floods like a happy stream,
While stubborn sprouts, they fiercely dream.
A spoonful here, a bite of that,
One uncle claims it's all pure fat.

Dessert table, a magical land,
Where pies and cakes all take their stand.
We raid the goods like it's a heist,
Leaving no pastry unturned, not even a slice.

With bellies full and hearts content,
We'll relive tales of time well spent.
So, raise a glass to foods divine,
And laugh aloud—this feast is mine!

Essence of Autumn's Bounty

Pumpkin pies on window sills,
Cranberry fights after the drills.
Kids sneak bites of turkey legs,
While grandma shows off her eggnog pegs.

Gravy rivers, flowing wide,
Uncle Joe has nowhere to hide.
He trips on shoes left in the way,
And falls in mashed potatoes, what a display!

Stuffing crammed in every nook,
A family read like an open book.
Watch the cat smell all the greens,
Dreams of turkey in fluffy scenes.

Laughter bubbles in warm embrace,
Every plate a silly race.
Dinner's done, but wait, oh dear,
There's room for pie—bring it here!

Candied Dreams and Roasted Hues

Sugar highs from candied yams,
Dance around like silly clams.
Aussie hats on the heads of mice,
Best friends eat and roll in rice!

Turkeys strut in kitchens bright,
While toddlers giggle at the sight.
Two pies each, it would be grand,
If only we had more plate land!

Silly screams over gravy spills,
Can't blame them, it's full of thrills.
Grandpa's snoring by three o'clock,
Sleepy eyes and belly rock.

Time to cheer, it's all in fun,
Eating battles have begun!
One more round, let's raise a toast,
To funny faces and summer's ghost!

The Spice of Togetherness

Silly hats and pumpkin spice,
Grandma's laughs, oh so nice.
Siblings bicker 'bout the pie,
Dad just hopes it's not too dry.

Taters dancing on the floor,
Everyone's sneaking a little more.
Auntie joins in with a jig,
As Uncle Bob sips from the big swig.

Flavors blend in merry slap,
Voices echo, laughter clap.
The feast awaits, the clock ticks fast,
Hope the turkey's not too vast!

When food hits the table, oh what glee,
We gobble up, in pure jubilee.
With every bite, a tale unwinds,
And funny memories in our minds.

Flavorful Echoes of Family

Cousins chase, their laughter bounces,
One's in the pantry, another's pounces.
Dinner rolls as flying hates,
Every toss breaks food debates.

Mashed clouds rise from every fork,
Like UFOs, they surely cork.
Sauce drips down, like free-fall magic,
Uncle Fred's face turns just tragic!

Tiny hands work on desserts,
Chocolate rivers down their shirts.
Never-ending bites of fun,
Can anyone have just one?

When at last the meals are done,
We sit and ponder all the fun.
A toast to chaos, and the mess we weave,
Thanksgiving echoes, we truly believe!

Flavors of Connection

The turkey's dance, it spins a tale,
While cousin Joe grabs the last pastry trail.
Potatoes sunbathe in butter's embrace,
As Grandma sneezes, the pie takes its place.

Scented laughter fills up the air,
With Uncle Bob's jokes, who really can bear?
We sip sweet cider, it's a wild delight,
While the dog eyes the feast, ready to bite.

Everyone's waiting with mouths all agape,
Except for dear dad, he's wrapped in a cape.
His superhero duty—gravy brigade,
He's saving the day, or so he has said.

The table's a riot, a glorious scene,
With dishes galore, and maybe a green?
As laughter erupts, we truly all find,
The best kind of flavors are love intertwined.

Warmth from the Oven

Oh, the oven's warmth, like a big cozy hug,
With cookies and pies, it's our family's drug.
Mom's secret spice, can't tell if it's sage,
Or last week's leftovers that caused this stage.

The rolls are rising, but so is the heat,
Dad's in charge now, we hide from defeat.
His apron is stained, a culinary war,
Cranberry splatters all over the floor.

The yams join the banquet, sweet and divine,
Though Cindy's still working on her wine.
A sip for the chef, a splash for the meal,
Will someone survive this Thanksgiving ordeal?

"Dinner is ready!" we all get in line,
Just one more slice of that pumpkin design.
It's a feast of mishaps, a dinner of fun,
Where the sideline cheers till the last drumstick's done.

Hearthside Hues of Gratitude

Gather 'round folks, hearth's glowing bright,
With mismatched chairs, oh what a sight!
Grandpa's turkey tales, we've heard them all,
Last year's still topped with that pickleball.

Stuffing surprises, what's hidden in there?
Cousins all chuckle, as bubbles declare.
A casserole's dance, it jiggles with cheer,
While Aunt Edna's hat holds a bass in a leer.

Caught in the chaos, a mishap unfolds,
The gravy's now swimming with tales that it holds.
Chasing that rogue, the rolls make a run,
Who knew a dinner could be this much fun?

So here's to the flavors, the laughter, the joy,
Ragtag connections no one can destroy.
With hearts full of gratitude, we all chime in,
Here's a toast to the chaos—let the games begin!

Paper Plates and Heartfelt Wishes

On paper plates, the dreams do glide,
With turkey towers and sweet potato pride.
The salad's a riot, tossed with a grin,
As we all compete to see who can win.

Uncle Ted's battles with the cranberry jam,
While Aunt Louise tries to keep cool, 'Oh, ham!'
The forks are drawn, and the stakes are high,
Who will claim the last piece of pie?

Kids are all giggling, the dog's in the fray,
While Dad's telling tales from his glorious day.
Between bites and burps, the chatter flows sweet,
As stories tumble like breadcrumbs beneath our feet.

So here's to the moments, the laughter we make,
On paper plates stacked up with care (and a shake).
With heartfelt wishes and full cups of cheer,
Let's feast on the fun, and not shed a tear!

Aromatic Gatherings

The turkey's roasting in a pan,
While Aunt May's cooking with her hands.
She spills the gravy, what a sight,
We laugh so hard, it feels so right.

Pumpkin pie sits on the shelf,
Dad stares at it, forgets himself.
He takes a slice, and oh, the cheer,
Looks like he's got pie on his ear!

Cousins clash in playful fights,
Who gets the drumstick? That ignites.
The table shakes, the chairs, they creak,
As dogs and kids both start to squeak.

What scents arise from pots and pans,
As everyone dances in their plans.
With every bite, a giggle blooms,
Thanksgiving's joy fills all the rooms.

A Symphony of Seasonal Scents

Onions sizzle, what a tease,
The cat swoops in with expert ease.
Mom yells, 'No! That's not for you!'
But whiskers twitch with every stew.

Cranberry sauce, so bright and tart,
Uncle Joe thinks it's art to start.
He globs some on, then with a frown,
Claims he created a 'berry crown.'

Mashed potatoes mount like a hill,
A mountain high, we all get our fill.
But wait, what's that? An alien plume?
A rogue green bean, now that's a doom!

As laughter swells amongst the feast,
We raise our glasses, to say the least.
Here's to the smells of joy and fun,
In this delightful, wacky run!

Whiffs of Gratitude

The rolls are rising, soft and round,
Grandpa's snores are the only sound.
He dreams of feasts, of gravy floods,
While we pile plates high with food floods.

The sweet potatoes with marshmallow peaks,
Look like a mountain, oh what cheek!
Cousin Tim takes a giant scoop,
And suddenly, he's in a soup!

Brussels sprouts begin to steam,
Mom says, "Please, just try one beam."
But Dad turns green, can't hold it in,
And then we all burst out in grins.

By the end, we're all a mess,
With crumbs and giggles, who could guess?
In every bite, a hug or two,
Thanksgiving's joy, so warm and true.

The Magic of Simmering Stews

In the kitchen, chaos reigns supreme,
Pots and pans join in a gleeful theme.
Sister stirs while brother dances,
Spills the broth, we all take glances.

Garlic wafts and tickles noses,
Mom's thick soup, everyone proposes.
Will it be magic? Or just a flop?
Either way, it's time to hop!

The dog looks up with hungry eyes,
As we feast, oh how he sighs.
He woofs at crumbs, his face a plea,
Uncle says, "Not for you, wee be!"

When the meal's done, we're rolling wide,
With full bellies, we all confide.
To laughter shared and tales retold,
Thanksgiving's warmth will never grow old.

Golden Browned Delights

Turkey struts with pride, wearing a glaze,
Cranberry sauce dances, in a sweet, tart maze.
Stuffing whispers secrets, of herbs and cheer,
While mashed potatoes ponder, "Is gravy near?"

Pumpkin pie at the end, looks oh-so-sweet,
But a cat sneaks a crumb, on silent feet.
The table's a stage, with dishes so bright,
Where cousins debate, who'll win the food fight!

Rolls puff up mighty, like little balloons,
While the dog dreams of treats, under the spoons.
A holiday feast, chaos wrapped in smiles,
Thanksgiving's a circus, with laughter in piles!

So raise up a glass, let the nonsense flow,
As we gather in joy, in sunshine and snow.
With family around, and love that's sincere,
It's a feast to remember, oh bring on the cheer!

Warmth in Every Bite

The turkey's so golden, it can't help but shine,
While grandma sneaks bites, thinking no one can spy.
Stuffing in abundance, a loaf on the side,
Somehow, Aunt Edna just thinks she's a guide.

Gravy's a river, flowing thick as molasses,
While kids figure out, who can fill their fat fasses.
The scent of sweet spices fills every nook,
And Uncle Joe's snoring, what a funny book!

Pumpkin pies gather like stars at a dance,
Each slice is a challenge, a dessert romance.
The laughter erupts, with every stuffed face,
As food fights break out, what a wild place!

So let's eat with gusto, no need to be shy,
For dinner's a race, not a slow, lingering pie.
With plates piled high, we will not take a break,
Oh, the joy of this meal, it's the laughter we make!

Feast for the Soul

A table adorned, with colors so bright,
Food piled high, what an outrageous sight.
The turkey's been dressed, with dignity grand,
While everyone wonders, "Who's bringing the brand?"

Mashed potatoes are fluffy, like clouds up above,
Gravy's a waterfall, a chef's kind of love.
The rolls are all resting, like pillows of glee,
As we tell tales that are funny, and free!

Green beans are snapping, with sweet smiles of joy,
While kids make a mess, like each one's a toy.
Aunts are a flurry, with tales from the past,
While uncles just nod, hope these moments will last.

So dive into laughter, forget all the fuss,
It's a feast for the soul, for all of us.
With bellies all full, and hearts even more,
We savor this chaos, it's worth every score!

Flavorful Embraces

On the table, a symphony, of flavors combined,
Turkey and gravy are perfectly aligned.
Cranberry fights back, oh what a bold stance,
While rolls start a riot, they just want to dance!

Each fork full of joy, a celebration of fun,
While kids swap their veggies, under the sun.
The laughter erupts, like popcorn in heat,
The brandy's so crafty, oh, what a sweet treat!

Desserts stand in line, like soldiers so proud,
As grandpa recounts tales, a growing crowd.
The chaos unfolds, in this joyful embrace,
Every laugh is a blessing, in this special place.

So toast to the flavors, let our voices unite,
In this funny commotion, everything feels right.
Together we feast, till we can eat no more,
On this day of thankfulness, who could ask for more?

Milton Keynes UK
Ingram Content Group UK Ltd.
UKHW030749121124
451094UK00013B/834